The Complete PANCHATANTRA

Asampreksha Karyatva   Ill-considered Action

Retold & illustrated by
Bujjai

© Bujjai
First published 1999
Second impression June 2000

Published by
Devamala Books Pvt Ltd

III Floor Zenofer Tower
No 119/2 Jawaharlal Nehru Road
Jafferkhanpet
Chennai 600083
Phone 3711824 3711825
Fax 0091 44 3712332
e-mail msmgroup@satyam.net.in

Designed by Krishna Shastri
Processed by Bee Vee Graphics, Chennai
Printed by Vadapalani Press,
AVM Compound, Vadapalani, Chennai 600026

To Lakshmi, my wife,

Who, for forty years,

stood by me through my struggles,

encouraged me in all my endeavours,

and left me and my children

suddenly two years ago,

I dedicate these books

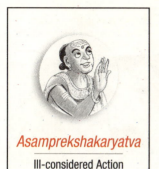

Asamprekshakaryatva

Ill-considered Action

THIS FINAL SECTION OF THE **PANCHATANTRA** ILLUSTRATES THE DIRE CONSEQUENCES OF THOUGHTLESS AND ILL-ADVISED ACTION!

TELL US THE STORY, SIR!

THERE ONCE LIVED A MERCHANT NAMED RATNAKARA WHO LOST ALL HIS ANCESTRAL WEALTH THROUGH BAD LUCK.

WHEN ONE'S WEALTH IS LOST, EVERYTHING IS LOST. ONE'S GOOD DEEDS ARE COMPLETELY FORGOTTEN.

EVEN ONCE-FRIENDLY NEIGHBOURS IGNORE SUCH UNFORTUNATES! IT'S A SHAME...

ONE DAY, THE POOR MERCHANT FELT SO MISERABLE THAT HE DECIDED TO END HIS LIFE. HE THEN FELL ASLEEP AND HAD A DREAM IN WHICH A GOLDEN FIGURE APPEARED...

WHO ARE YOU?

DON'T YOU KNOW ME?

NO!

I'M THE INEXHAUSTIBLE RICHES OF YOUR ANCESTORS. YOU CAN MAKE ME RETURN!

DON'T PUT AN END TO YOUR LIFE. DO AS I BID YOU!

YES, SIR!

TOMORROW I'LL VISIT YOUR HOUSE IN THE FORM IN WHICH I APPEAR NOW.

THEN?

THEN TAKE A CLUB AND STRIKE MY HEAD HARD WITH IT AND I'LL BE TRANSFORMED INTO A BIG MASS OF GOLD.

THE FIGURE THEN DISAPPEARED AND THE MERCHANT WOKE UP...

OH, WHAT A DREAM! IF IT WERE ONLY TRUE...

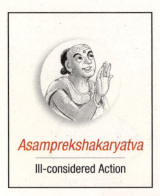

Asamprekshakaryatva

Ill-considered Action

THE NEXT MORNING...

IF DREAMS COME TRUE, WHAT IS REAL LIFE?

AFTER SOME TIME, WHEN A BARBER WAS GIVING HIM A SHAVE...

GRACIOUS GOD! AM I STILL DREAMING? THE SAME FIGURE IN THE SAME YELLOW ROBE?

WHAT SHALL I DO NOW? SHOULD I SMASH THE HEAD OF THIS HOLY MAN?

WITH AN UNWILLING MIND AND A TREMBLING HAND, THE MERCHANT TOOK A STOUT CLUB AND HIT HIM HARD ON THE HEAD...

LO AND BEHOLD! THE MONK DISAPPEARED AND IN HIS PLACE STOOD A MOUND OF SHINY GOLD COINS.

MIRACULOUS! HOW THE DREAM HAS COME TRUE!

SO THIS IS THE WEALTH OF MY FOREFATHERS!

THE BARBER HAD WITNESSED ALL THIS WITH MUCH INTEREST...

DEAR FELLOW! DON'T TELL ANYBODY ABOUT WHAT YOU JUST SAW

I WON'T, I PROMISE!

HERE, TAKE THIS!

THE BARBER WENT HOME AND THOUGHT DEEPLY ABOUT WHAT HAD HAPPENED.

YES, THAT'S IT! WHEN A MONK OR SADHU IS STRUCK ON THE HEAD WITH A CUDGEL, HE TURNS INTO GOLD!

I KNOW A MONASTERY WHERE A WHOLE LOT OF MONKS LIVE!

THE NEXT DAY, THE BARBER WENT TO THE OUTSKIRTS OF THE CITY, WHERE THE SADHUS LIVED...

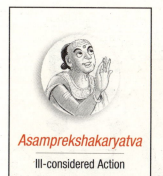

Asamprekshakaryatva

Ill-considered Action

HOLY SIRS! PLEASE STEP INTO MY HOUSE AND BLESS ME!

NO! DON'T YOU KNOW WE HAVE GIVEN UP ALL DESIRE AND BROKEN ALL TIES?

I HUMBLY BESEECH YOU TO STEP INTO MY HOUSE FOR A MOMENT AND GRACIOUSLY ACCEPT MY OFFERINGS!

SO THE SADHUS FOLLOWED THE BARBER TO HIS HOUSE...

HOLY SIR! PLEASE COME IN ONE AT A TIME SO THAT I CAN HONOUR YOU ALL TO MY SATISFACTION!

SO THE FIRST SADHU ENTERED HIS HOUSE. A STOUT CUDGEL HAD BEEN PROPPED UP IN A CORNER...

THE BARBER TOOK IT UP AND...

...AND STRUCK EACH MONK IN TURN WITH HIS CUDGEL...

HOLY SIR! IT'S NOW YOUR TURN.

TO HIS UTTER DISMAY, THEY DID NOT TURN INTO GOLD--ONE SWOONED AND THE OTHERS YELLED LOUDLY FOR HELP.

HELP! HELP! HELP!

WHAT'S THE COMMOTION? LET'S FIND OUT!

5

Asamprekshakaryatva

Ill-considered Action

THE KING'S SOLDIERS BROKE INTO THE BARBER'S HOUSE AND AFTER FINDING OUT WHAT HAD HAPPENED, TOOK THE BARBER TO THE KING...

WHY HAVE YOU ATTACKED THESE HOLY MEN?

YOUR MAJESTY! I WAS ONLY IMITATING RATNAKARA!

WHO IS HE? WHAT DID HE DO?

THE BARBER TOLD THE KING WHAT HAPPENED IN RATNAKARA'S HOUSE: HOW A SADHU, WHEN STRUCK ON HIS HEAD, HAD TRANSFORMED INTO A HEAP OF GOLD. THEN THE KING ORDERED HIS SOLDIERS TO BRING THE MERCHANT TO HIM.

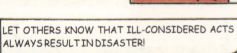

IN THE KING'S PRESENCE...

WHY DID YOU KILL A SADHU?

SIRE! I HAVE NEVER KILLED ANY SADHU. PERMIT ME TO TELL YOU WHAT REALLY HAPPENED.

THEN RATNAKARA NARRATED THE WHOLE STORY: WHAT HE HAD DREAMT, AND HOW HIS ANCESTRAL WEALTH HAD COME BACK TO HIM IN THE FORM OF A MONK...

THIS BARBER IS A RASCAL AND SHALL BE HANGED FOR HIS THOUGHTLESS DEED.

LET OTHERS KNOW THAT ILL-CONSIDERED ACTS ALWAYS RESULT IN DISASTER!

THIS REMINDS ME OF THE STORY OF THE HOUSEWIFE AND THE MONGOOSE...

PRAY, TELL US THE STORY, SIRE!

ONCE, THERE LIVED IN A TOWN A BRAHMIN NAMED DEVASARMA, WHOSE WIFE WAS RAISING THEIR BABY SON AND A MONGOOSE WITH EQUAL LOVE AND CARE.

52/137

Asamprekshakaryatva

Ill-considered Action

ONE DAY, IN THE BRAHMIN'S HOUSE...

MY DEAR! I'M GOING TO FETCH WATER FROM THE RIVER. PLEASE LOOK AFTER OUR BOY TILL I RETURN!

DON'T WORRY, DEAR! HE IS SLEEPING PEACEFULLY IN THE CRADLE.

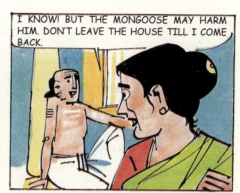

I KNOW! BUT THE MONGOOSE MAY HARM HIM. DON'T LEAVE THE HOUSE TILL I COME BACK.

HOW SILLY A DOTING MOTHER IS!

AFTER SOME TIME, THE BRAHMIN ALSO LEFT THE HOUSE TO BEG FOR FOOD...

A BLACK SNAKE CREPT INTO THE HOUSE, AND MOVED SLOWLY TOWARDS THE CRADLE...

HE MAY BITE MY LITTLE BROTHER. I'LL STOP HIM.

I MUST KILL HIM!

HISS!

THE LOYAL MONGOOSE LEAPT AT THE SNAKE, FOUGHT WITH HIM AND TORE HIM TO PIECES.

THE VENOMOUS RASCAL IS DEAD! NOW I MUST RUN TO MOTHER WITH THIS GOOD NEWS!

THE MONGOOSE RAN TO THE RIVER IN PRIDE AND JOY. THE BRAHMIN'S WIFE SAW HIM WITH BLOOD TRICKLING OUT OF HIS MOUTH...

MERCIFUL GOD! WHAT HAS HE DONE TO MY BOY?

HE MUST HAVE KILLED HIM! UNGRATEFUL WRETCH!

Asamprekshakaryatva
Ill-considered Action

IN A BLIND RAGE, THE WOMAN HIT THE MONGOOSE HARD WITH THE PITCHER, KILLED HIM AND RAN HOME IN PANIC...

MY CHILD! MY CHILD! WHERE ARE YOU?

MY DARLING! YOU ARE ALIVE!

WHAT DO I SEE HERE? MY GOD! MY GOD! WHAT HAVE I DONE? WHAT A WRETCH I AM!

THE MONGOOSE SAVED HIS LITTLE BROTHER. I, HIS MOTHER, KILLED HIS SAVIOUR IN THOUGHTLESS ANGER.

MEANWHILE, HER HUSBAND HAD RETURNED HOME AND SAW WHAT HAD HAPPENED...

IF YOU HAD ONLY STAYED AT HOME, THIS WOULDN'T HAVE HAPPENED. MY THOUGHTLESSNESS AND YOUR GREED HAVE BROUGHT ABOUT THIS CALAMITY!

THE WRETCHED WOMAN TOLD HER GRIEF-STRICKEN HUSBAND THE STORY OF THE FOUR FORTUNE-HUNTERS...

ONCE, IN A VILLAGE, THERE LIVED FOUR FRIENDS. THEY WERE VERY POOR.

ONE DAY...
POVERTY IS A CURSE. IT IS THE CAUSE OF ALL THE MISERY IN THIS WORLD.

A PERSON MAY HAVE GOOD LOOKS, INTELLECT, COURAGE AND SCHOLARSHIP, YET IF HE IS POOR, HE IS NEITHER HAPPY NOR RESPECTED.

IT'S BETTER TO DIE THAN TRY TO BE POVERTY-STRICKEN.

YES, YOU'RE RIGHT! WEALTH ALONE BRINGS HAPPINESS...

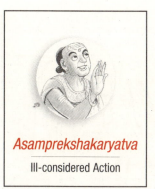

Asamprekshakaryatva

Ill-considered Action

HOW CAN WE GET SOME MONEY?

THERE ARE EVER SO MANY WAYS: BEGGING, LENDING MONEY AT HIGH INTEREST, FAWNING AND FLATTERY IN A KING'S COURT, TILLING LAND, TRADE AND SO ON.

WHICH WAY SHALL WE CHOOSE?

ROYAL GRACE ISN'T STEADY. AGRICULTURE IS LABORIOUS. BEGGING IS MEAN...

LENDING MONEY IS RISKY AND WE'VE NOTHING TO LEND!

HA! HA! HA!

HENCE TRADE IS THE ONLY WAY FOR US.

HOW CAN WE PROSPER IN TRADE?

ADULTERATION, FALSE WEIGHTS AND BALANCES, ABNORMAL INCREASE OF PRICES AND SO ON...

BUT EVEN TO TRADE WE REQUIRE MONEY! FOREIGN TRAVEL IS THE ONLY WAY LEFT TO US!

YES!

YES!

THE FOUR FRIENDS THEN SET OUT ON THEIR JOURNEY TO FOREIGN LANDS IN SEARCH OF WEALTH...

ON THEIR WAY, THEY MET AN ASCETIC WHO WAS REALLY A WIZARD...

HOLY SIR! WE FALL AT YOUR FEET!

GET UP, MY SONS!

YOU'RE THE GRACIOUS GOD APPEARING BEFORE US IN THIS HUMAN FORM.

Asamprekshakaryatva

III-considered Action

WHAT IS YOUR WISH?

WE ARE POOR PILGRIMS SEEKING OUR FORTUNE. BLESS US AND SHOW US A WAY TO ACQUIRE WEALTH.

I'M PLEASED WITH YOU, MY CHILDREN! TAKE THESE MAGIC FEATHERS, ONE FOR EACH OF YOU, AND...

GO NORTH TOWARDS THE HIMALAYAS...

AND THEN, SIR?

WHEREVER A FEATHER FALLS, THERE ITS OWNER MUST DIG AND HE'LL FIND TREASURE.

THANK YOU, SIR!

OVERJOYED, THE FOUR FORTUNE-HUNTERS TOOK THE FEATHERS AND STARTED OFF ON THEIR JOURNEY. ON THEIR WAY...

AH! MY QUILL HAS DROPPED TO THE GROUND.

LET'S DIG HERE AND SEE WHAT HAPPENS!

THEY DUG THE GROUND EAGERLY, AND LO AND BEHOLD...

THE SOIL IS ALL COPPER!

I'M LUCKY, INDEED!

IT'S ONLY COPPER, AND COPPER IS A CHEAP METAL. LET'S PROCEED FURTHER!

NO! I'M CONTENT WITH THIS, YOU GO ON WITHOUT ME!

THE OTHERS CONTINUED THEIR JOURNEY TILL ANOTHER QUILL DROPPED.

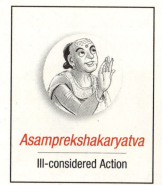

Asamprekshakaryatva

III-considered Action

THEY DUG INTO THE GROUND...

AH! WE'VE FOUND SILVER! HOW LUCKY I AM!

MY FRIENDS! PLEASE SHARE THIS WEALTH WITH ME!

NO! WE'LL GO FURTHER!

THE TWO FRIENDS CONTINUED ON...

ANOTHER QUILL FELL, AND, AGAIN, THE FRIENDS DUG INTO THE EARTH...

GOLD! BY ALL THAT'S WONDERFUL, IT'S GOLD!!

LET'S SHARE IT, MY FRIEND!

NO, THANKS, I'M GOING FURTHER...

WHAT FOR?

DON'T YOU SEE? IT WAS FIRST COPPER, THEN CAME SILVER AND NOW, GOLD.

ISN'T IT EVIDENT THAT MY MAGIC QUILL WILL FETCH ME PRECIOUS STONES? COME WITH ME!

NO, NO! I'LL WAIT HERE TILL YOU RETURN.

THE LAST OF THE FORTUNE-SEEKERS CONTINUED ON HIS JOURNEY.

DAY AND NIGHT, HE TRUDGED ON, WEARY AND THIRSTY...

Asamprekshakaryatva

Ill-considered Action

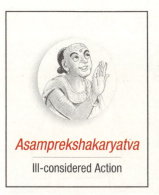

Asamprekshakaryatva

Ill-considered Action

MEANWHILE, THE MAN WHO HAD FOUND GOLD WAITED FOR HIS FRIEND'S RETURN AND STARTED OFF IN SEARCH OF HIM.

Asamprekshakaryatva

III-considered Action

THEN HIS FRIEND NARRATED THE STORY OF THE FOUR FRIENDS TO THE WHEEL-BEARER.

ONCE, THERE LIVED FOUR FRIENDS IN A CITY. THREE OF THEM WERE GREAT SCHOLARS BUT THEY LACKED COMMON SENSE.

THE FOURTH WAS NO SCHOLAR BUT WAS BLESSED WITH COMMON SENSE.

ONE DAY...
WHAT GOOD IS OUR SCHOLARSHIP WHEN IT IS NOT PUT TO ANY USE?

WE'VE EARNED NEITHER WEALTH NOR FAME IN THIS WORTHLESS PLACE.

LET'S LEAVE THIS CITY AND TRAVEL TO FOREIGN LANDS.

SO, THE FOUR FRIENDS SET OUT ON THEIR JOURNEY...

ON THE WAY...
YOU KNOW ONE OF US WON'T BE OF ANY USE IN OUR ADVENTURE. WHY SHOULD HE TAKE A SHARE OF WHAT WE EARN?

YOU'RE RIGHT! LET'S SEND HIM BACK!

MY FRIEND! YOU DON'T FIT INTO THE COMPANY OF SCHOLARS LIKE US. WHY DON'T YOU GO HOME?

Asamprekshakaryatva

Ill-considered Action

THAT IS BAD! WE SHOULD NOT TURN HIM AWAY, HE MAY NOT BE A SCHOLAR BUT HE IS OUR FRIEND.

YOU'RE RIGHT! LET HIM COME WITH US AND HAVE HIS SHARE OF WHAT WE GET.

THEN THE THREE SCHOLARS, ACCOMPANIED BY THEIR SIMPLE FRIEND, PROCEEDED ON THEIR JOURNEY...

THEY WERE SOON PASSING THROUGH A FOREST...

LOOK! BONES!

I'M SURE THEY BELONG TO A DEAD LION!

RIGHT! LET'S NOW PUT TO TEST OUR KNOWLEDGE AND BRING THEM BACK TO LIFE.

PLEASE LISTEN TO ME, MY FRIENDS!

WILL YOU SHUT UP! WE'RE IN NO MOOD TO LISTEN TO A FOOL!

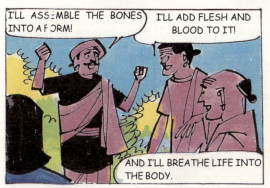

I'LL ASSEMBLE THE BONES INTO A FORM!

I'LL ADD FLESH AND BLOOD TO IT!

AND I'LL BREATHE LIFE INTO THE BODY.

STOP IT! IT'S RISKY. IF IT REALLY HAPPENS, THE LION WILL KILL US ALL!

DON'T INTERFERE WITH OUR GREAT EXPERIMENT!

THEN WAIT FOR A FEW SECONDS. LET ME CLIMB A TREE AND SAVE MYSELF.

Asamprekshakaryatva

Ill-considered Action

THE THREE SCHOLARS PROCEEDED WITH THEIR FOOLISH EXPERIMENT. THEY BROUGHT BACK THE LION BACK TO LIFE, AND, OF COURSE, IT SPRANG UPON AND DEVOURED THEM...

THANK GOODNESS I DON'T POSSESS SCHOLARSHIP WHICH IS DEVOID OF COMMON SENSE!

THE GOLD-FINDER CAME TO THE END OF HIS STORY...

IT'S USEFUL TO HAVE COMMON SENSE! IT CAN SAVE YOU FROM DEATH.

I DON'T QUITE AGREE WITH YOU. EVEN COMMON SENSE CANNOT HELP YOU IF FATE WILLS OTHERWISE.

I'LL TELL YOU A STORY WHICH ILLUSTRATES THIS TRUTH.

PLEASE TELL ME!

THERE LIVED THREE FRIENDS IN A LAKE. TWO WERE FISH, SAHASRABUDHI AND SATABUDHI, AND THE THIRD WAS A FROG, SWALPABUDHI.

ONE DAY...

HUSH!

I WONDER WHO THEY ARE!

THIS LAKE IS FULL OF FISH. LET'S COME TOMORROW AND CATCH THEM.

GOD HELP US! DID YOU HEAR THAT? LET'S LEAVE THIS PLACE BEFORE THEY RETURN!

HA! HA! MY FRIEND, DON'T BE AFRAID. HOW ARE YOU SO SURE THEY'LL COME BACK?

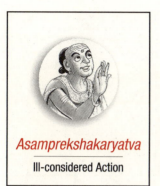

Asamprekshakaryatva

Ill-considered Action

EVEN IF THEY DO, WE'LL USE OUR WITS AND SAVE OURSELVES AND YOU.

THIS IS WHERE WE WERE BORN. WE CAN'T LEAVE ON A MERE SUSPICION!

I'M NOT WISE AND INTELLIGENT LIKE YOU TWO. I CANNOT REASON WITH YOU BOTH!

BUT I FEEL I MUST LEAVE THIS PLACE AT ONCE. SO, FAREWELL, MY FRIENDS!

ALL RIGHT, MY FRIEND! WE SEE YOU'RE NOT WILLING TO TAKE OUR ADVICE.

THE NEXT MORNING, THE FISHERMEN CAME TO THE LAKE AND CAUGHT ALL THE FISH IN THE LAKE AND SAHASRABUDHI AND SATABUDHI WERE ALSO KILLED...

ALAS! MY WISE FRIENDS COULD NOT SAVE THEMSELVES.

THE WHEEL-BEARER FINISHED HIS STORY...

SO EVEN INTELLIGENCE MUST ULTIMATELY YIELD TO FATE.

TRUE! TRUE! BUT WE SHOULD ALSO LISTEN TO A FRIEND'S ADVICE.

YOUR GREED AND YOUR ARROGANCE CLOUDED YOUR BRAIN.

LISTEN, I'LL TELL YOU A STORY!

ALL RIGHT!

Asamprekshakaryatva

III-considered Action

THE GOLD-FINDER BEGAN HIS STORY...

ONCE, THERE LIVED A DONKEY NAMED GARVI. ONE DAY HE MET A JACKAL AND MADE FRIENDS WITH HIM.

ONE MOON-LIT NIGHT...

LOOK AT THAT ORCHARD, MY FRIEND! IT IS FULL OF DELICIOUS FRUIT! LET'S GO THERE AND FEAST ON THEM!

ALL RIGHT, BUT YOU MUST BE QUIET!

THE TWO ENTERED THE ORCHARD AND ATE TO THEIR HEARTS' CONTENT...

HOW WONDERFULLY HAPPY I AM! A SUPERB MEAL AND THIS MOONLIGHT...

ONLY ONE THING IS LACKING NOW TO MAKE IT ALL PERFECT!

WHAT'S THAT?

MUSIC, HEAVENLY MUSIC!

YES! YOU'RE RIGHT. BUT HOW CAN WE GET IT NOW?

STRANGE, INDEED! YOU DON'T SEEM TO KNOW THAT YOUR OWN FRIEND IS A RENOWNED MUSICIAN!

I'LL ENTERTAIN YOU WITH MY MELODIOUS VOICE!

NO! PLEASE, NOT NOW! FOR HEAVEN'S SAKE!

DO YOU DOUBT MY MUSICAL TALENT?

NO, NOT AT ALL! BUT WE'RE TRESPASSERS. A LOVER AND A THIEF MUST CARRY ON THEIR AFFAIRS QUIETLY!

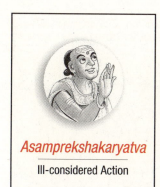

Asamprekshakaryatva

Ill-considered Action

THERE IS AN OLD SAYING THAT A MAN WHO SNEEZES CAN NEVER BECOME A SUCCESSFUL THIEF!

I'M AFRAID YOUR VOICE WILL BE TOO LOUD FOR THIS TIME AND PLACE.

DON'T BE SILLY! YOU'VE NO EAR FOR MUSIC.

FORGET ABOUT MY TASTES. IT IS DANGEROUS FOR YOU TO SING NOW. IT MAY WAKE UP THE FARMERS.

NO! YOU CAN'T STOP ME! THIS MOONLIGHT INSPIRES ME SO!

ALL RIGHT! BUT WAIT TILL I REACH A SPOT FROM WHERE I CAN SEE THE FARMERS COMING!

BRAYAAHAAA! BRAHAHA!

HOW DISTRESSING! GOD HELP HIM!

BRAY AAHAA!! BRA! BRAYAHH BRAAHAAH

ON HEARING THE DONKEY BRAY, THE FARMERS WOKE UP AND RUSHED TO THE ORCHARD. THEY BEAT HIM UP, TIED A BIG STONE TO HIS NECK AND LEFT. THEN THE JACKAL APPROACHED HIS FRIEND, THE DONKEY...

MY DEAR GARVI! YOUR PERFORMANCE WAS SUPERB. HAVE THE FARMERS HONOURED YOU WITH THAT TOKEN WHICH HANGS FROM YOUR NECK?

THEY'RE FOOLS WHO CAN'T APPRECIATE MUSIC!

THE GOLD-FINDER CONCLUDED THE STORY THUS:

THEREFORE, ONE SHOULD HEED A FRIEND'S ADVICE.

TRUE! TRUE!

Asamprekshakaryatva

Ill-considered Action

ONE SHOULD ALWAYS ACT UPON THE GOOD ADVICE OF A FRIEND. I'M REMINDED OF THE STORY OF MANDA...

WHO WAS HE?

A WEAVER.

ONE DAY, HE WENT TO A FOREST NEAR HIS VILLAGE IN SEARCH OF WOOD TO MAKE PEGS FOR HIS LOOM.

THIS TREE LOOKS GOOD. I'LL GET PLENTY OF WOOD FROM IT.

HE LIFTED HIS AXE TO CUT IT DOWN, WHEN HE HEARD A VOICE...

PLEASE STOP! THIS TREE IS MY HOME. DON'T CUT IT DOWN.

I NEED WOOD FOR MY LOOM, SO I'M CUTTING IT DOWN...WHO ARE YOU?

I'M THE TREE FAIRY. IF YOU LEAVE THIS TREE ALONE, I'LL GRANT YOU ANY BOON YOU ASK OF ME.

PLEASE LET ME CONSULT MY FRIEND AND MY WIFE ABOUT THE BOON!

THE WEAVER WENT STRAIGHT TO A TRUSTED FRIEND, AND TOLD HIM WHAT THE TREE FAIRY HAD SAID...

GO BACK AND ASK FOR A KINGDOM. I SHALL BE YOUR CHIEF MINISTER.

ALL RIGHT!

LET ME CONSULT MY WIFE ALSO.

NO, NO, DON'T DO THAT!

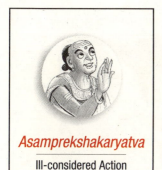

Asamprekshakaryatva

Ill-considered Action

NEVER SEEK THE COUNSEL OF A WOMAN. GIVE HER GOOD FOOD, FINE CLOTHES AND BEAUTIFUL JEWELS...

BUT NEVER TAKE HER ADVICE!

WHY NOT?

BECAUSE WOMEN ARE SELFISH.

MY WIFE IS DIFFERENT. SHE IS GENTLE AND SELFLESS, IT IS MY DUTY TO SEEK HER COUNSEL.

THE WEAVER HASTENED HOME AND SOUGHT HIS WIFE'S ADVICE...

HOW LUCKY! ASK FOR ANOTHER PAIR OF HANDS AND A SECOND HEAD FOR YOUR BODY!

WHAT FOR?

YOU'RE A WEAVER. WITH TWO PAIRS OF HANDS, YOU CAN MANAGE TWO LOOMS AT ONCE!

AND OUR EARNINGS WILL BE DOUBLED!

WONDERFUL! EXCELLENT!

THE FOOLISH WEAVER HURRIED TO THE TREE AND DECLARED HIS WISH...

AND THE TREE FAIRY GRANTED IT...

HOW LUCKY, INDEED! WITH FOUR HANDS AND TWO HEADS, I'LL SOON BECOME RICH!

LOOK AT THAT!

WHAT STRANGE CREATURE IS THAT?

Asamprekshakaryatva

III-considered Action

THE WHEEL-BEARER ENDED HIS STORY THUS:

WHEN THE VILLAGE FOLK SAW THE WEAVER WITH FOUR HANDS AND TWO HEADS THEY THOUGHT HE WAS A MONSTER AND BEAT HIM TO DEATH.

SO, ONE SHOULD ACCEPT GOOD ADVICE, AND ACT ON IT.

I'M HAPPY YOU NOW AGREE WITH ME.

ALL THIS MISERY IS THE RESULT OF MY GREED. THIS REMINDS ME OF A STORY!

LET ME HEAR IT.

THERE ONCE LIVED A BEGGAR WHO USED TO GO FROM DOOR TO DOOR AND COLLECT FOOD.

I'M LUCKY TODAY. EVEN AFTER LUNCH, I'VE PLENTY OF FOOD LEFT IN THIS POT.

THE POOR FELLOW WAS SO OVERJOYED THAT HE SOON FELL INTO A DAY-DREAM.

A FAMINE WILL STRIKE THE LAND. PEOPLE WILL DIE OF HUNGER...

A RICH MAN WILL OFFER AT LEAST A HUNDRED GOLD PIECES FOR THIS FOOD...

WITH THAT MONEY, I'LL BUY A COW AND SELL ITS MILK AND THEN I'LL BUY MORE COWS, AND SO ON...

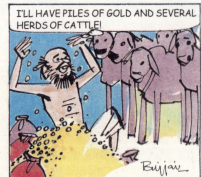

I'LL HAVE PILES OF GOLD AND SEVERAL HERDS OF CATTLE!

Asamprekshakaryatva

Ill-considered Action

THE BEGGAR DREAMED ON...

THEN I'LL BUY HORSES AND ALSO AN ELEPHANT. A RICH MAN WILL THEN COME TO ME AND SAY...

SIR! WILL YOU PLEASE MARRY MY DAUGHTER? I'LL GIVE YOU ONE HALF OF MY WEALTH AS DOWRY.

SOON, I'LL HAVE A BEAUTIFUL SON.

HIS NAME SHALL BE CHANDRAHASA.

ONE DAY, WHEN I'M BUSY WITH MY ACCOUNTS, THE CHILD WILL COME AND DISTURB ME.

I'LL GET ANGRY AND SCOLD MY WIFE.

MY DEAR, COME HERE AND TAKE THIS CHILD AWAY. I'M BUSY.

WAIT A MOMENT!

ARROGANT WOMAN! OBEY ME AT ONCE OR I'LL KICK YOU!

THE WHEEL-BEARER CAME TO THE END OF HIS STORY:

THE BEGGAR IN HIS TRANCE KICKED HIS POT OF FOOD AND THE DAY-DREAM...

...CAME TO A SAD END.

ONE SHOULDN'T BE EXCESSIVELY GREEDY AND DREAM OF THINGS WHICH CAN NEVER HAPPEN. HAVEN'T YOU HEARD THE STORY OF CHANDRAKETU, THE GREEDY?

NO, WHO WAS HE?

Asamprekshakaryatva

III-considered Action

ONCE, THERE LIVED A KING NAMED CHANDRAKETU. HE HAD A SON FOR WHOSE AMUSEMENT HE KEPT A PACK OF MONKEYS AND A FLOCK OF SHEEP...

AMONG THE MONKEYS, THERE WAS AN OLD AND WISE ONE WHICH CLOSELY OBSERVED EVERYTHING THAT HAPPENED AT COURT...

MY DEAR FELLOWS! LOOK AT THAT RAM. HE VISITS THE ROYAL KITCHEN AND DEVOURS WHATEVER HE SEES THERE!

SO WHAT?

THE COOKS WILL ONE DAY GET FURIOUS AND MAY HIT HIM WITH ANYTHING THAT IS HANDY.

SO WHAT? IT'LL TEACH HIM A LESSON.

ONE DAY, THE COOKS MAY CATCH HOLD OF A BURNING LOG AND HIT HIM WITH IT!

IT WILL SERVE HIM RIGHT!

YOU DUNDERHEADS! THE WOOL ON THE SHEEP'S BACK WILL IMMEDIATELY CATCH FIRE.

SO WHAT?

HE WILL THEN RUN WILDLY ALL OVER THE PLACE. THE THATCHED STABLE NEARBY WILL CATCH FIRE AND THE HORSES IN THERE WILL BE BURNT...

WONDERFUL IMAGINATION! AND THEN?

FOOLS! DON'T YOU KNOW THAT MONKEY'S FAT IS THE BEST BALM FOR BURNS ON HORSES.

THE KING WON'T HESITATE TO PUT AN END TO OUR LIVES FOR THE SAKE OF THE HORSES.

ABSURD! SHEER NONSENSE!

I'M SURE IT WILL HAPPEN ONE DAY!

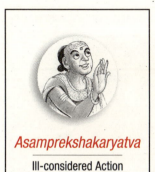

Asamprekshakaryatva

Ill-considered Action

LET'S GET OUT OF HERE BEFORE IT'S TOO LATE!

LIKE ALL OLD PEOPLE, YOU'RE SENILE. YOU SEEM TO HAVE LOST YOUR BEARINGS...

WE'RE USED TO THE DELICIOUS DAINTIES OF THE ROYAL KITCHEN. WE CAN'T LIVE IN A FOREST.

UNABLE TO CONVINCE HIS KINSFOLK OF THE IMPENDING DANGER, THE OLD MONKEY LEFT THE PALACE FOR A FOREST...

BLESSED IS HE WHO DOES NOT WITNESS THE DEATH OF HIS DEAR ONES, THE MISFORTUNES OF FRIENDS, THE TREACHERY OF HIS WIFE AND THE RUIN OF HIS COUNTRY...

AND SOON THE OLD MONKEY'S PREDICTIONS CAME TRUE: THE SHEEP RAN OUT OF THE KITCHEN WITH ITS COAT ON FIRE, AND RAN INTO THE STABLE. THE FIRE SPREAD, AND THE HORSES WERE SCORCHED. SO THE MONKEYS WERE KILLED FOR THEIR FAT TO BE USED AS BALM FOR THE HORSES...

THIS NEWS SOON REACHED THE OLD MONKEY...

WHAT A HEINOUS CRIME. IT BREAKS MY HEART.

IT'S UNFORGIVABLE. I MUST DO SOMETHING!

WITH A BURNING DESIRE FOR VENGEANCE, HE WANDERED ABOUT THE FOREST AND CAME TO A LAKE...

I'M THIRSTY...WAIT A MINUTE!

THESE FOOT PRINTS ARE STRANGE. THEY LEAD INTO THE LAKE BUT NOT ONE OF THEM COMES OUT.

THERE MUST BE A MONSTER IN THIS LAKE!

SO THE CLEVER MONKEY USED A LOTUS STALK AS A STRAW AND DRANK THE WATER THROUGH IT.

Asamprekshakaryatva

Ill-considered Action

WHILE THE OLD MONKEY WAS DRINKING WATER A MONSTER APPEARED OUT OF THE LAKE...

SIR, I ADMIRE YOUR WISDOM! NO ONE WHO ENTERS THIS LAKE SURVIVES.

I SHALL GRANT YOU A BOON! NAME ONE!

HERE'S A GOLDEN OPPORTUNITY TO TAKE REVENGE!

SIR! HOW MANY MEN CAN YOU SWALLOW AT A TIME?

THOUSANDS! BUT THEY SHOULD STEP INTO THE WATER.

SIR, GRANT ME A NECKLACE FOR A SHORT TIME. WITH ITS HELP, I CAN GET YOU PLENTY OF FOOD.

HERE YOU ARE!

ARMED WITH THE PEARL NECKLACE, THE OLD MONKEY WENT TO THE CITY...

LOOK! LOOK AT THAT MONKEY!

WHAT A PRECIOUS NECKLACE HE HAS ON!

HEY, YOU! WHERE DID YOU GET THAT FROM?

THERE IS A LAKE IN YONDER FOREST. WHOEVER TAKES A DIP IN IT IS REWARDED WITH A NECKLACE LIKE THIS.

SOON, THE KING CAME TO HEAR OF THE STORY. AT ONCE, HE RAN TO THE OLD MONKEY WHO REPEATED HIS TALE...

WONDERFUL! I'LL TAKE ALL MY FOLLOWERS TO THE LAKE AND COLLECT THOUSANDS OF NECKLACES!

Asamprekshakaryatva

Ill-considered Action

EXCELLENT IDEA! FOLLOW ME, THEN, O KING!

THE CLEVER MONKEY LED THE GREEDY KING AND HIS FOLLOWERS TO THE LAKE...

GREED FOOLS EVERYONE, EVEN KINGS AND SCHOLARS...

SIR! LET YOUR FOLLOWERS JUMP NOW INTO THE LAKE, ALL TOGETHER. WE'LL JUMP IN WHEN THEY RETURN.

AT THE KING'S COMMAND, ALL HIS FOLLOWERS DIVED INTO THE LAKE...

...AND WERE GOBBLED UP AT ONCE BY THE MONSTER.

THE KING WAS HORROR-STRICKEN. THE MONKEY CLIMBED QUICKLY UP A TREE...

WHAT IS THE MEANING OF THIS? WHAT HAVE YOU DONE!

MERCILESS KING! ONCE, YOU DESTROYED THE LIVES OF ALL MY PEOPLE. YOU ARE REPAID NOW IN YOUR OWN COIN!

I'VE SPARED YOUR LIFE TO TEACH YOU A LESSON.

THE PENITENT KING LEFT THE PLACE IN SORROW. THE MONSTER THEN APPEARED OUT OF THE WATER...

MY CLEVER FRIEND, YOU'VE TAKEN REVENGE UPON YOUR ENEMY, AND YOU'VE APPEASED MY HUNGER!

KEEP THE NECKLACE AS A TOKEN OF OUR FRIENDSHIP!

THE GOLD-FINDER CAME TO THE END OF HIS STORY:

THE GREEDY DO NOT LISTEN TO GOOD ADVICE AND SO ARE RUINED IN THE END...

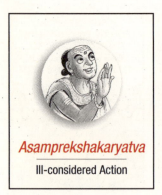

Asamprekshakaryatva

Ill-considered Action

LET ME NOW BID YOU FAREWELL, MY FRIEND!

IS IT PROPER TO ABANDON A FRIEND IN DISTRESS?

NO! BUT I CAN NEITHER SEE YOU SUFFER NOR HELP YOU!

I'M ALSO AFRAID TO HELP YOU NOW!

WHY?

SOME EVIL MAY BEFALL ME AS WELL...THIS REMINDS ME OF A STORY...

LET ME HEAR IT!

ONCE, THERE WAS A KING NAMED VIJAYASENA WHO HAD A LOVELY DAUGHTER, MAUKTIKA.

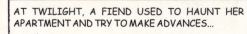

AT TWILIGHT, A FIEND USED TO HAUNT HER APARTMENT AND TRY TO MAKE ADVANCES...

...BUT COULD NOT CARRY HER OFF AS THE PRINCESS WAS SAFE IN A MAGIC CIRCLE.

ONE DAY, WHEN THE PRINCESS WAS SPENDING TIME WITH A FRIEND...

WHAT IS THE MATTER WITH YOU? YOU TREMBLE LIKE A LEAF IN THE WIND!

MY FRIEND! LOOK IN THAT CORNER!

WHAT IS IT? I DON'T SEE ANYTHING!

CAN'T YOU SEE IT? IT'S A FIEND!

MY GOD!

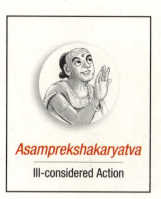

Asamprekshakaryatva

III-considered Action

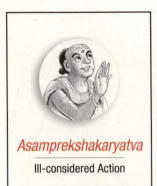

Asamprekshakaryatva

Ill-considered Action

THE HORSE GALLOPED LIKE LIGHTNING, AND THE RIDER WAS UNABLE TO CONTROL IT...

HE **HAS** TO BE AN EVIL SPIRIT! HOW TO GET RID OF HIM?

HE IS WHIPPING ME REALLY HARD! HOW SHALL I GET RID OF HIM?

MERCIFUL GOD! SAVE ME FROM THIS SPIRIT.

AT THIS JUNCTURE, THE THIEF GRABBED HOLD OF A TREE...

LUCKY I COULD CLING ON!

I'M FREE! I MUST RUN AWAY.

A MONKEY SITTING ON THE TREE SAW WHAT HAD HAPPENED. HE WAS THE FIEND'S FRIEND...

MY FRIEND! WHY HAVE YOU TAKEN THE FORM OF A HORSE?

WHY DO YOU RUN AWAY FROM A MERE MAN...EAT HIM!

ON HEARING THESE WORDS, THE SPIRIT ASSUMED HIS NATURAL FORM AND RETURNED.

MEAN-WHILE, THE THIEF...

THIS MONKEY HAS NO BUSINESS TO INTERFERE LIKE THIS!

I'LL TEACH HIM A LESSON!

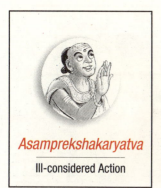

Asamprekshakaryatva

Ill-considered Action

THE ANGRY THIEF TOOK THE MONKEY'S TAIL IN HIS GRIP, AND BIT IT HARD.

OW!

OHHO OHOH!!

OH, MY GOD! SEE HE'S VERY POWERFUL! SEE HOW HE CHEWS THE MONKEY'S TAIL!

I MUST RUN AWAY!

THE GOLD-FINDER CAME TO THE END OF THE STORY: THE FOOLISH FIEND WAS DECEIVED BY THE MONKEY'S LOOK OF HORROR...

...THOUGHT THE THIEF WAS A MIGHTIER SPIRIT THAN HIMSELF AND FLED IN SHEER FRIGHT.

MY FRIEND! I SIMPLY CAN'T BEAR THE PAIN I SEE IN YOUR FACE.

GOODBYE!

PRAY, DON'T LEAVE ME IN THIS PLIGHT!

NO ONE CAN HELP YOU. ONE MUST SUFFER FOR ONE'S THOUGHTLESS DEEDS.

61-202

NO, IT IS FATE THAT DECIDES ONE'S FORTUNES.

HAVEN'T YOU HEARD THE STORY OF THE FORTUNATE PRINCESS?

NO!

ONCE, THERE LIVED A KING NAMED MADHUSENA. HIS DAUGHTER WAS BORN WITH A HORN ON HER FOREHEAD...

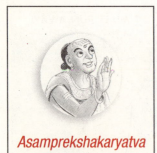

Asamprekshakaryatva

Ill-considered Action

THE KING WAS HORRIFIED BY THIS AND SUMMONED HIS MINISTER TO CONSULT HIM.

IT'S A GREAT MISFORTUNE TO HAVE A DAUGHTER WITH A HORN ON HER FOREHEAD.

WHAT SHOULD WE DO?

SHALL WE PUT AN END TO HER LIFE...OR...?

NO, WE SHOULD NOT ACT IN HASTE! LET US TAKE THE ADVICE OF OUR PRIESTS.

THEY ARE WISE, LIKE THAT BRAHMIN OF YORE.

WHO WAS HE? WHAT WAS HIS STORY?

ONCE UPON A TIME, A BRAHMIN WAS TRAVELLING THROUGH A FOREST WHEN A FIEND SAW HIM FROM THE TOP OF A TREE.

AH!

THIS FELLOW WILL SERVE MY PURPOSE NOW.

THE BRAHMIN SOON APPROACHED THE TREE AND THE FIEND JUMPED ONTO HIS SHOULDERS.

OH!

WHAT'S THIS? WHO ARE YOU?

HAHH!

AHHA! I'M THE GREAT KING OF FIENDS. NOW WALK ON!

OH!

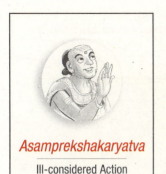

Asamprekshakaryatva

Ill-considered Action

MY GOD! I'M DOOMED!

THE FRIGHTENED BRAHMIN WALKED ON WITH THE FIEND ON HIS SHOULDERS. AFTER SOME TIME...

IT'S STRANGE! THE FIEND'S FEET ARE AS SOFT AS BUTTER...

MY DEAR SIR! IF YOU DON'T MIND, MAY I ASK YOU A QUESTION?

GO AHEAD. ASK AWAY!

SIR! YOUR FEET ARE TENDER, LIKE LOTUS FLOWERS...WHY IS THAT?

LONG AGO, I TOOK A VOW NOT TO TOUCH THE GROUND UNTIL I WASHED MY FEET IN YONDER LAKE...

I CAN'T WALK NOW AS MY FEET CAN'T TAKE IT.

SIR! I SHALL GLADLY TAKE YOU THERE.

HMMM. THIS GIVES ME AN IDEA!

THEY SOON APPROACHED THE LAKE.

HEY! TAKE ME TO THE VERY EDGE OF THE LAKE.

NOW, YOU STAY HERE ON THE BANK TILL I WASH MY FEET AND OFFER PRAYERS TO MY GOD.

ALL RIGHT!

POOR FELLOW! HE DOESN'T KNOW THAT HE WILL BE KILLED AFTER MY BATH...

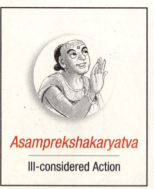

Asamprekshakaryatva

Ill-considered Action

I'M SURE HE'LL KILL ME WHEN HE RETURNS...

I'LL RUN AWAY! HE DARE NOT FOLLOW ME.

THE MINISTER ENDED HIS STORY:

SO, THE CLEVER BRAHMIN FORESAW THAT THE FIEND COULDN'T PURSUE HIM BEFORE HIS BATH BECAUSE OF HIS VOW...

...AND ACTED PROMPTLY AND SAVED HIMSELF.

SO LET'S CONSULT OUR PRIESTS BEFORE WE ACT.

AND THE PRIESTS WERE SUMMONED IMMEDIATELY.

SIR! IT WILL BE CALAMITOUS TO KEEP HER HERE.

IT WILL BRING DEATH TO THE FATHER AND TO HER HUSBAND.

WHAT SHALL WE DO THEN?

NEVER LOOK UPON HER. MARRY HER OFF TO SOMEONE

...AND SEND THE COUPLE OUT OF THIS COUNTRY

MEANWHILE, LOCK HER UP IN AN APARTMENT...

SO THE KING ISSUED A PROCLAMATION THROUGHOUT HIS KINGDOM.

Bijjai

Asamprekshakaryatva

Ill-considered Action

CITIZENS! HERE IS A PROCLAMATION!

HIS MAJESTY, THE KING, OFFERS THE HAND OF HIS DAUGHTER AND ONE HUNDRED THOUSAND GOLD MOHURS TO ANYONE WHO COMES FORWARD TO MARRY HER!

BUT HE MUST IMMEDIATELY LEAVE THIS COUNTRY WITH HER FOR GOOD!

THE PRINCESS HAS A HORN ON HER FOREHEAD.

WHOEVER MARRIES HER COURTS DEATH!

WHO WANTS TO LEAVE HIS NATIVE LAND?

MANY YEARS PASSED. THE PRINCESS WAS NOW A YOUNG WOMAN BUT NO ONE CAME FORWARD TO MARRY HER.

ONE DAY, TWO FRIENDS, A HUNCHBACK AND A BLIND MAN CAME TO KNOW ABOUT THIS.

LET'S GET THE GOLD WHICH THE KING IS OFFERING.

OUR DAYS OF POVERTY WILL END. WE'LL BE HAPPY EVEN THOUGH WE MAY NOT LIVE LONG.

63/206

TO HIM WHO IS HUNGRY, ALL OF LIFE'S PLEASURES SEEM WORTHLESS.

I'LL MARRY THE PRINCESS AND WE SHALL LIVE HAPPILY WITH THE GOLD.

THAT'S A GREAT IDEA!

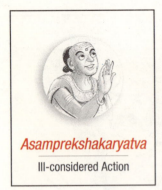

Asamprekshakaryatva

Ill-considered Action

IN THE KING'S PRESENCE...

MAY IT PLEASE YOUR MAJESTY, THERE IS A BLIND MAN WHO IS WILLING TO MARRY THE PRINCESS!

REALLY? BRING HIM HERE!

SIRE! I AM READY TO MARRY THE PRINCESS!

ALL RIGHT! MAKE ARRANGEMENTS FOR THE WEDDING IMMEDIATELY!

AND SO THE PRINCESS WAS MARRIED TO THE BLIND MAN...

...AND THEY WERE SENT TO A DISTANT LAND. THE HUNCHBACK WENT WITH THEM.

...AND ALL THREE LIVED HAPPILY WITH THE GOLD.

ONE DAY...

PRINCESS! I PITY YOU!

WHY?

YOU'RE MARRIED TO SOMEONE WHO CAN'T EVEN SEE YOU!

IT IS FATE'S DECREE!

WE CAN GET RID OF THE BLIND FELLOW AND LIVE HAPPILY TOGETHER...HERE'S A PLAN.

Asamprekshakaryatva

Ill-considered Action

AFTER A FEW DAYS...

LOOK HERE!

OH!

THIS BLACK SNAKE'S VENOM IS DEADLY..

SO?

COOK IT WITH LOTS OF SPICE, AND TURN IT INTO A TASTY DISH.

WHAT FOR?

FEED IT TO THE BLIND FELLOW AND HE'LL DIE.

OH, NO! I'M AFRAID!

DON'T BE SILLY! IF WE KILL HIM OFF, WE CAN LIVE HAPPILY EVER AFTER!

MEANWHILE, I HAVE TO GO TO TOWN TO ATTEND TO SOMETHING.

THE PRINCESS FOLLOWED THE INSTRUCTIONS OF THE HUNCHBACK AND STARTED COOKING THE SNAKE.

MY DEAR, I'M COOKING A RARE FISH FOR YOU TODAY!

THAT'S VERY KIND OF YOU!

PLEASE STIR IT NOW AND AGAIN WITH THIS SPOON WHILE I BRING WATER FROM THE WELL.

THE BLIND MAN WENT ON STIRRING THE POT WHEN, SUDDENLY, SOMETHING MIRACULOUS HAPPENED...

WHAT IS HAPPENING?

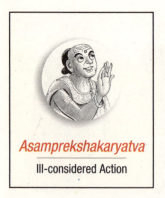

Asamprekshakaryatva

Ill-considered Action

THE POISONOUS VAPOURS ISSUING FROM THE VESSEL HAD CURED HIS BLINDNESS!

BY ALL THAT'S WONDERFUL, I CAN SEE! MY BLINDNESS IS GONE!

MY GOD! WHAT'S THIS?

THIS IS NO FISH. IT'S A DEADLY SNAKE!

AHA! SOMEONE WANTS TO KILL ME...LET ME WAIT AND SEE...

AFTER SOME TIME, THE PRINCESS AND THE HUNCHBACK RETURNED. THE BLIND MAN WAS STILL STIRRING THE POT...

HAVE YOU COOKED THE FISH AND FED YOUR HUSBAND?

IT'S NOT YET READY.

YOU SWINE! SO THIS IS HOW YOU WANTED TO GET RID OF ME!

WHAT ARE YOU SAYING? I DON'T UNDERSTAND!

REALLY? THEN MAYBE THIS WILL BRING LIGHT TO YOU!

STOP! SPARE ME!

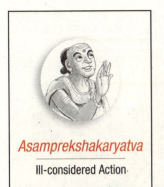

Asamprekshakaryatva

Ill-considered Action

THE WHEEL-BEARER CAME TO THE END OF HIS TALE...

THE HUSBAND, IN UTTER RAGE, HIT THE HUNCHBACK WITH A CLUB. WITH THE BLOW, HIS HUNCH DISAPPEARED...

HE THEN HIT HIS WIFE ON HER FOREHEAD AND THE HORN BROKE OFF.

AND, THEREAFTER, THE HUSBAND AND HIS PENITENT WIFE LIVED HAPPILY EVER AFTER.

WHAT YOU SAY IS TRUE BUT NEVER RELY ON FATE ALONE. ACT WITH WISDOM!

AND, MY DEAR FRIEND, DON'T BE SO GREEDY.

GOODBYE!

VISHNU SHARMA CAME TO THE END OF **ASAMPREKSHAKARYATVA**, THE FIFTH AND FINAL PART OF THE **PANCHATANTRA**, THUS...

SO, ILL-CONSIDERED ACTION RESULTS IN DANGER AND SUFFERING.

LISTEN TO ADVICE, BUT WEIGH ITS PROS AND CONS. ACT WISELY, MY DEAR PRINCES!

WE'VE NOW COME TO THE END OF THE **PANCHATANTRA**. LET US RECOLLECT IN BRIEF WHAT IT HAS TAUGHT US.

YES, SIR!

MITRABEDHA, THE FIRST **TANTRA**, TELLS US HOW A KING WAS RUINED BY PAYING HEED TO TWO GREEDY AND SCHEMING COUNSELLORS.

Asamprekshakaryatva

Ill-considered Action

IN THIS STORY, TWO CLEVER JACKALS, KARATAKA AND DAMANAKA...

DESTROY THE FRIENDSHIP OF PINGALAKA, THE LION KING, AND SANJIVAKA, THE BULL, FOR THEIR OWN ENDS.

FROM THIS TALE, YOU LEARN ABOUT DIVIDING YOUR ENEMIES AND VANQUISHING THEM.

BUT YOU MUST MAKE SURE YOU DON'T FALL INTO THE SAME TRAP!

YES, SIR! WE'LL BE SURE TO REMEMBER THIS.

THE SECOND **TANTRA**, **MITRALABHA**, ILLUSTRATES HOW FOUR WISE FRIENDS, LAGHUPATANAKA, HIRANYAKA, MANTHARA AND CHITRANGA...

...OVERCAME ALL DIFFICULTIES BY STANDING TOGETHER THOUGH THEIR MEANS WERE LIMITED.

STAND UNITED ALWAYS. NEVER FALL OUT WITH FRIENDS. THEN NO DANGER CAN BEFALL YOU.

THE THIRD PART IS **SANDHIVIGRAHA**. IT TEACHES US HOW TO FACE THE ENEMY AND OVERCOME HIM.

THE FORETHOUGHT OF THE OLD CROW, THE WISE COUNSELLOR OF MEGHAVARNA, THE KING OF CROWS, BRINGS VICTORY TO HIM AND RUIN TO HIS ENEMY.

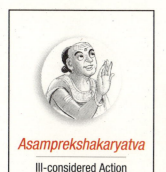

Asamprekshakaryatva

Ill-considered Action

THROUGH STRATEGY, THE CROWS WIPE OUT THE OWLS!

NOW, PRINCES! TELL ME ABOUT **LABDHANASA**, THE FOURTH **TANTRA**!

IT TELLS US THE STORY OF KRAKACHA THE CROCODILE: HOW HE WAS OUTWITTED BY BALIVARDA, THE MONKEY, AND HOW HE LOST WHAT HE HAD GAINED.

FOLLY AND INDISCRETION TAKE AWAY FROM YOU THE ADVANTAGES YOU ALREADY POSSESS.

THE FIFTH **TANTRA** TELLS US THAT EXCESSIVE GREED AND ILL-CONSIDERED ACTION RESULT IN PAIN AND PERIL.

GOOD! I'M HAPPY WITH YOUR PROGRESS, MY DEAR PRINCES!

SHALL WE GO TO THE KING, YOUR FATHER, AND SHOW HIM WHAT YOU HAVE LEARNT?

YES, SIR!

IN KING SUDARSHANA'S APARTMENTS...

SIRE! I'VE BROUGHT YOUR SONS BACK TO YOU. THEY ARE NOW WELL-VERSED IN STATECRAFT!

THEY'RE NOW THE WORTHY SONS OF A GREAT KING!

LET ME OFFER MY GRATEFUL THANKS TO YOU, REVERED SIR. I HAVE A HUMBLE REQUEST...

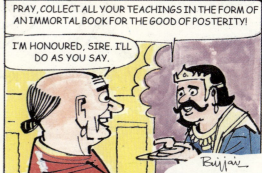

PRAY, COLLECT ALL YOUR TEACHINGS IN THE FORM OF AN IMMORTAL BOOK FOR THE GOOD OF POSTERITY!

I'M HONOURED, SIRE. I'LL DO AS YOU SAY.

CHARACTERS FROM MITRABEDHA

DAMANAKA

KARATAKA

SANJIVAKA

PINGALAKA

CHARACTERS FROM **MITRALABHA**

CHARACTERS FROM **SANDHIVIGRAHA**

UPAMARDA

HIRANYAKA

LAGHUPATA-NAKA

CHITRANGA

MEGHAVARNA

MANTHARA

CHIRANJEEVI